To all my family an
I am grateful and thankfi

.

I am grateful and thankful to the moments that inspired me to
write and dream.

I am grateful and thankful to the life.

Thank you God for these blessings.

POEMS

Traveller

TRAVELLER

Traveller knows, Travellers goes, Traveller dreams,
He seeks, he sweeps, he does not respect any peaks.

The ordinary people have plenty of "Can't",
The Traveller has a plenty of land.
He doesn't respect any borders,
And doesn't take any orders.

The Traveller knows when to start,
Because he listens only to his heart.
The heart is the key, you better believe,
Otherwise, you will never something achieve.

If you have a dream, if you have a goal,
Go and pursue it, make your own law.
It will not be easy, of course,
But this is the Traveller's energy source.

If you ever look deep at the traveller's eyes,
You will see how the fires from there arise.
This is the power of places he's already been.
Can you understand me now, what I mean?

Travelling doesn't care about your gender or skin,
But it does care to hold up your chin.
Do you have all of this imagination and inspiration?
Go, be a Traveller, and choose your destination.

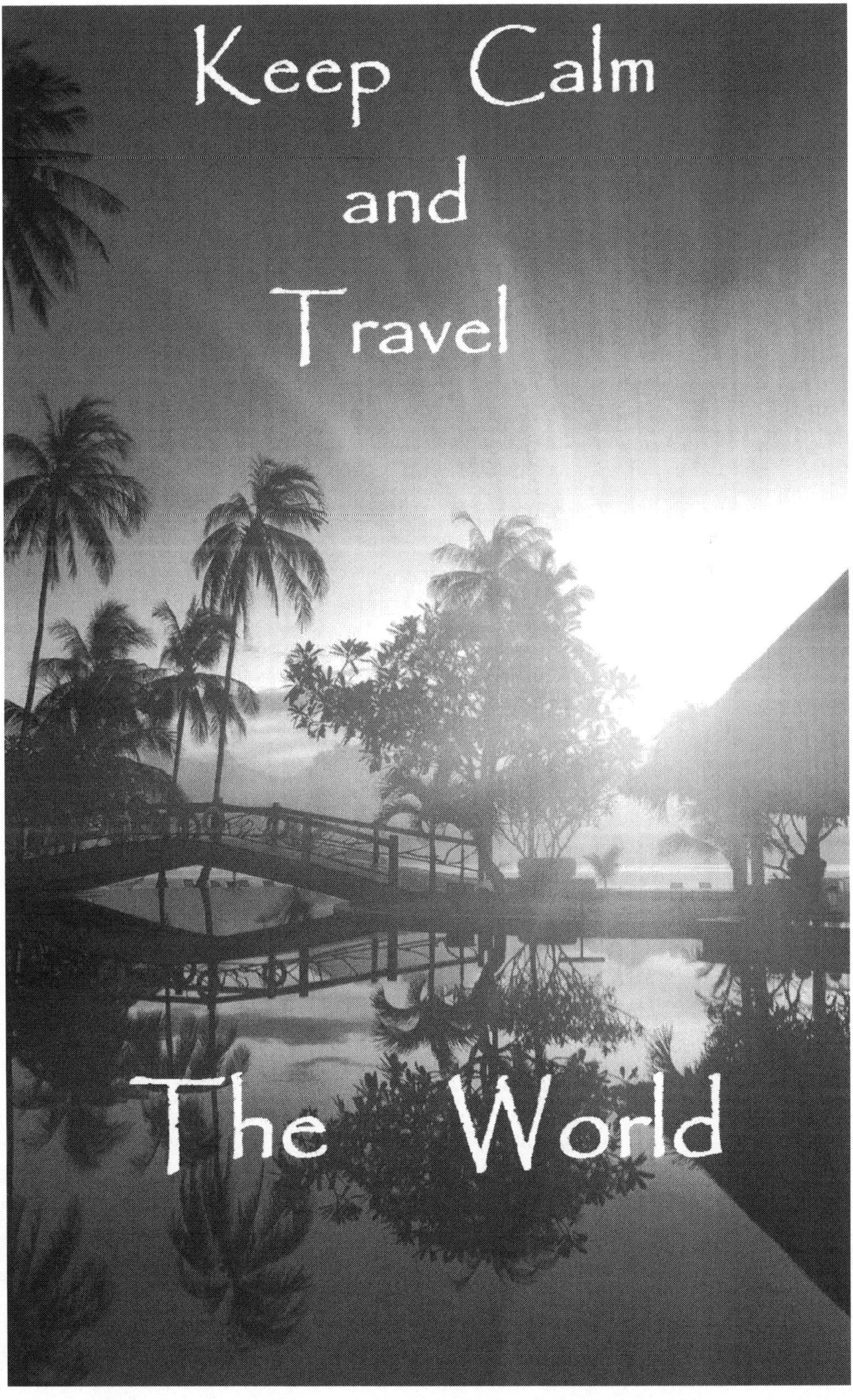
Keep Calm
and
Travel
The World

KEEP CALM AND TRAVEL THE WORLD

Choose a track, take your snack!
Pack the bag, and don't look back!
Call a friend, release the bend,
Go, travel to the end!

The world is waiting,
This is out of doubt,
It is time to go, and start the count!

One planet, 7 continents, 196 countries, you've got!
Go and hit them by your mighty shot!
The clock is ticking, you already know,
It is time to run your own show.

There are powerful places you have to see and feel,
Never forget, you're the master of your wheel!
Forget about the excuses and delays,
It's about your dreams, you have to chase!
Always there is a way, always there is a direction,
Go, point the country, put it in your collection.

Many times speechless, you will be,
Realizing that you're born truly free!
The words powerless you will feel,
And you will be stronger than the steel!
This is the mighty power the traveling has,
When you sense it once, you won't pray for less.

Looking the airplanes at the sky, never will be the same.
Because, you already possess the biggest flame.
After every journey nothing is the same,
And you can't wait to start another one again!

It's all about attitude and mind,
Or people who prefer to stay blind.
One life, one planet, one mission,
Exploring the world is my prime ambition.

Take your faith, your courage, and forget about the fear!
Go, climb a hill, see the stars, feel the wind, and I will give you a beer!
Don't wait for the next week, a month, or an year.
KEEP CALM AND TRAVEL THE WORLD today, my dear!

PATIENCE

PATIENCE

One of the hardest tests in life is the patience to wait,
This I state without any debate!
Sometimes the time you will hate,
But you should never stop to maintain your faith.

Waiting could be unbearable, I know,
The time could be harmful, torturing, and slow,
Your desire could burn you inside,
These are all things you can't hide.

But there is something that I know too,
The time will pass and you will look through,
In this tiny moment, your persistence will define the man you are,
Your struggle, your progress, and your shiny star.
Stubbornness, consistency and valor you need,
Only by them, you will notch up your deed.
But your mental fortitude and virtue to wait,
These are the things that make you great
.

By the time you wait many times you will fall and rise,
And every time you will receive a prize.
Sometimes the prize you will not see,
But you should know, you haven't fought for free.

Something vital, you should never forget.
On your way you can open every gate,
Only if you never surrender and you're willing to wait,

This is your life, this is your time, this is how you look,
Your heart should be the pen by which you write your book!

TIME

Again I'm taking the pen,
And I don't need any coffee to stimulate my brain.
This time I am going to write about the time,
I intend to touch you by my magic rhyme.

Many people are afraid of the hands of the clock,
They think, they scramble, but they don't want to talk.
Any of them has his own reason behind,
But it's a wistful story when they prefer to stay blind.

Thinking about the time, we have two choices in front,
They determine our actions, life, and the accomplishing that what we want.
Choice one is to struggle and fight with the time, building a wall,
Choice two is to smile, enjoy and live it all!
Which option to choose, it depends on you,
But let me first explain you my humble view.

Our time is something what we fully possess,
Don't try to deny this, cause you won't have any success.
This is my definition of the time,
This is how I perceive it, live it, and make it mine.

86 400 - this number to remember forever, I dare you,
Never let it out of your head, I command you.
These digits consist the seconds we have each day,
But we forget so often about them, and let them go away.
These seconds are limited, but our happiness is not,
We can make them fortunate and joyful, hitting them by one shot.

Our greatest asset in life is our time,
And we possess the power to make it shine.
Not money, but time you spend with the people you love,
Smile with them, play with them, and never put things above!
Sometimes this so vital advice you will neglect,
But I'll share with you the secret that will keep you correct.
A secret so simple and obvious at first,
But if you omit it, it makes your life worst.
Never forget, you are the time, and the time is you,
How you spend it, it depends on you.
This was my smooth and humble view,
If you want to debate it, take the pen, and show me your clue!

Hard

Work

HARD WORK

Dear Hard Work, I used to hate you!
When I've heard your name I run away from you.
Party was my best friend, not you.
Excuses and delays,
Sways and timeless holidays,
My life was full of Fridays.

Dear Hard Work, I used to hate you!
I've been afraid of your name,
Thus, I procrastinated my aim.
I've been afraid of failure,
So I didn't change my behavior.
I've been afraid of trying,
Therefore, I was always hiding.
But most, I was afraid of the pain,
Refusing your reign.

Ooh, Dear Hard Work,
I really used to hate you!
My eyes were closed for you,
And I didn't take my due.
My mind was confined,
How could I be so damn blind?
But there was someone who was waiting for you,
Someone who everything knew!
Someone who was ready to start,
This, someone, was my Heart.
The Heart knew you're somewhere there,
Waiting to change me forever.

Dear Hard Work, I don't longer hate you!
I love you! I need you!
I've broken the cycle, and I'm not stopping now,
I never will be down, and I am taking your crown!
I'm purifying my heart, taking my part,
And I am ready to start!
Patience, fortitude, humility, and faith,
This is how my destiny I'll create.

Dear Hard Work, I love you, and I am not longer afraid!
I have you in my heart, and I'll destroy any gate!
You're my attitude, discipline, and light,
Because of you, I found, I can write!
You're the foundation of my power, dignity, and soul,
You're my passion and spirit, which now I control!
From that moment listening to my Heart is a must,
BECAUSE IN THE HARD WORK I TRUST!

Manifestation of The Faith

MANIFESTATION OF THE FAITH

Have you ever wondered about the sense of your life,
And what is that thing that keeps your drive?
What's that thing that you can feel but can't see,
And what is that thing that makes you feel free?

You are wondering now, "Is this love?",
I'll tell you, "you're close but is one idea above".
You'll ask me then, "Is it about my friends?",
You are close again, but it has deeper sense.
You'll shout loudly, "It must be the money?"
But you've never been more away from it, honey.

I dare you now, set yourself on fire,
And then you will feel my desire.
I'm writing this words by my inspiration,
And my mission is to touch your imagination.
I want to remind you what a powerful weapon you have in your heart,
Because this is the way I create my art.

This is not just a poem, it is a manifestation of the Faith,
And what remarkable deeds, it can create.
The Faith is the source of your motivation,
And keeps you away from any frustration.

The Faith of one can change his life,
The Faith of few can defeat a strife,
The Faith of many can lead them to reward,
The Faith of one nation can change the world!

Our history is full of Faith,
So many battles, so many conquests, I can state.
Achilles, Gandhi, Jesus, Joan of Arc,
In our life, they have made the greatest mark.
Facing the enemy they've never been afraid
Because of their courage, bravery, and Faith.

Sweat on his face, flames in his eyes,
He fights to the end, and can't be surprised.
Determined spirit, vigorous soul,
He feels the victory and has all the control.
He knows when to stop, he knows when to start.
This is the man with Faith in his heart.

Tell me at the end,
What is that common thing among Ceaser, Napoleon, Joan of Arc, and Alexander the Great?
I think you already know it, this is the FAITH!

ALASKA

There is a statement I want to do,
Because this is my primary due.
There are places out there created from God,
If you want to see and explore them,
You must go against the odd.
When you witness them once,
You will be never the same,
The fire comes and also the flame.
The eyes are opened and the heart is beating,
Then you realize that the Greatness you're meeting.
Here I stop to write,
Because Alaska is a state of mind!

Mountains

THE MOUNTAIN

The Mountain can test,
But also does manifest.
The Mountain can't obey,
But can help you showing you the way.
The Mountain can't give absolution,
But it can allude the solution.
The Mountain can make you feel weak.
But the Mountain can lead also to the peak.
The Mountain can dominate,
But also it keeps your fate.
The Mountain can stumble,
But also it's humble.
The Mountain can inspire,
The Mountain is desire.

SISTERS

SISTERS

Something special, I would like to write,
But, NO - without anyone to cite!
These words are coming straight from the heart,
And from my very consciousness, mind, and esteem, they are a part.

I am a happy man, I can state,
Because, this very special moment, I managed to create.
Walking with my sisters somewhere in Milan,
Without to think, without to rush, without to plan.

The sun was shining, we've been together,
That's the only thing that HAS and WILL matter.
Yes, it is simple, but the life is simple too,
To be grateful and humble, it is our primary due.

Appreciation and gratitude are values, also, so needed,
It is where the soul and the spirit are conceded.
The life is short and only the moments, we possess,
There is nothing else here to confess.

I am a happy man, again, I will state!
In the true values of life, I have faith.
Yes, the life goes on, and we all grow,
But, there is only one thing, I need to know.
Happiness is simple, and here is the key,
It is having my loved ones next to me.

Dream Chaser

DREAM CHASER

I am a Dream Chaser,
And I want to represent an idea,
But before to read it let out your fear,
The fear is an enemy created by you,
It's not the thing you have to pursue.
I want to take you for a while to one miracle place,
The kingdom of your dreams I dare you to chase.

There only two keys, pain and belief,
They're the pure path for your soul to relieve.
I embrace them both, no matter how hard it seems,
Because this is the way, I chase my dreams.

I am a Dream Chaser, look at in my eyes!
There is no place for fear or either for a tear,
I won that war because of the weaknesses, I had before.
I've been broken once, but now I am a whole,
I've been hurt, and, therefore, I've grown.
I've been down, but now I am in my crown.
I've been crushed, I've been mad, I've been sad,
Therefore, now I cant'be stopped.
I've felt alone!
But, therefore, now I am solid like a stone.

Where focus goes energy flows,
This is what every Dream Chaser knows.
Like every beginning, you may not have the resources, money or education,
But you must let your faith to make the foundation.
Don't hesitate to want, don't hesitate to believe,
This is how everything you will achieve.

I am a Dream Chaser, and have a heart!
Remember the keys, pain and belief?
My heart is the place, where they're concieved.
This is my life, this is my time, this is how I look.
My heart is the pen by which I write my book.

The End